> Perhaps this is the moment for which you have been created
>
> Esther 4:14

An RMJ Journal

Copyright © 2017 Rogena Mitchell-Jones
Perhaps This Is the Moment - A Christian Journal
A Scripture Theme Journal - Esther 4:14
Rogena Mitchell-Jones — RMJ Journals

Simplicity.

An RMJ Journal

RMJ Manuscript Service LLC
www.rogenamitchell.com

College Rule Edition

All rights reserved.

ISBN-13: 978-1546740148
ISBN-10: 1546740147

*For if you remain completely silent at this time,
relief and deliverance will arise for the Jews from another place,
but you and your father's house will perish.
Yet who knows whether you have come to the kingdom
for such a time as this?"*

Esther 4:14 (NKJV)

Perhaps this is the moment for which you have been created.

...for such a time as this.

Perhaps this is the moment for which you have been created.

...for such a time as this.

Perhaps this is the moment for which you have been created.

...for such a time as this.

Perhaps this is the moment for which you have been created.

...for such a time as this.

Perhaps this is the moment for which you have been created.

...for such a time as this.

Perhaps this is the moment for which you have been created.

...for such a time as this.

Perhaps this is the moment for which you have been created.

...for such a time as this.

Perhaps this is the moment for which you have been created.

...for such a time as this.

Perhaps this is the moment for which you have been created.

...for such a time as this.

Perhaps this is the moment for which you have been created.

...for such a time as this.

Perhaps this is the moment for which you have been created.

...for such a time as this.

Perhaps this is the moment for which you have been created.

...for such a time as this.

Perhaps this is the moment for which you have been created.

...for such a time as this.

Perhaps this is the moment for which you have been created.

...for such a time as this.

Perhaps this is the moment for which you have been created.

...for such a time as this.

Perhaps this is the moment for which you have been created.

...for such a time as this.

Perhaps this is the moment for which you have been created.

...for such a time as this.

Perhaps this is the moment for which you have been created.

...for such a time as this.

Perhaps this is the moment for which you have been created.

...for such a time as this.

Perhaps this is the moment for which you have been created.

...for such a time as this.

Perhaps this is the moment for which you have been created.

...for such a time as this.

Perhaps this is the moment for which you have been created.

...for such a time as this.

Perhaps this is the moment for which you have been created.

...for such a time as this.

...this is the moment for which you have been created.

...for such a time as this.

Perhaps this is the moment for which you have been...

...for such a time as this.

Perhaps this is the moment for which you have been created.

...for such a time as this.

Perhaps this is the moment for which you have been created.

...for such a time as this.

Perhaps this is the moment for which you have been created.

...for such a time as this.

Perhaps this is the moment for which you have been created.

...for such a time as this.

Perhaps this is the moment for which you have been created.

...for such a time as this.

Perhaps this is the moment for which you have been created.

...for such a time as this.

Perhaps this is the moment for which you have been created.

...for such a time as this.

Perhaps this is the moment for which you have been created.

...for such a time as this.

Perhaps this is the moment for which you have been created.

...for such a time as this.

Perhaps this is the moment for which you have been created.

...for such a time as this.

Perhaps this is the moment for which you have been created.

...for such a time as this.

Perhaps this is the moment for which you have been created.

...for such a time as this.

Perhaps this is the moment for which you have been created.

...for such a time as this.

Perhaps this is the moment for which you have been created.

...for such a time as this.

Perhaps this is the moment for which you have been created.

...*for such a time as this.*

Perhaps this is the moment for which you have been created.

...for such a time as this.

Perhaps this is the moment for which you have been created.

...*for such a time as this.*

Perhaps this is the moment for which you have been created.

...for such a time as this.

Perhaps this is the moment for which you have been created.

...for such a time as this.

Perhaps this is the moment for which you have been created.

...for such a time as this.

Perhaps this is the moment for which you have been created.

...for such a time as this.

Perhaps this is the moment for which you have been created.

...for such a time as this.

Perhaps this is the moment for which you have been created.

...for such a time as this.

Perhaps this is the moment for which you have been created.

...for such a time as this.

Perhaps this is the moment for which you have been created.

...for such a time as this.

Perhaps this is the moment for which you have been created.

...for such a time as this.

Perhaps this is the moment for which you have been created.

...for such a time as this.

Perhaps this is the moment for which you have been created.

...for such a time as this.

Perhaps this is the moment for which you have been created.

...for such a time as this.

Perhaps this is the moment for which you have been created.

...for such a time as this.

Perhaps this is the moment for which you have been created.

...for such a time as this.

Perhaps this is the moment for which you have been created.

...for such a time as this.

Perhaps this is the moment for which you have been created.

...for such a time as this.

Perhaps this is the moment for which you have been created.

...for such a time as this.

Perhaps this is the moment for which you have been created.

...for such a time as this.

Perhaps this is the moment for which you have been created.

...for such a time as this.

Perhaps this is the moment for which you have been created.

...for such a time as this.

Perhaps this is the moment for which you have been created.

...for such a time as this.

Perhaps this is the moment for which you have been created.

...for such a time as this.

Perhaps this is the moment for which you have been created.

...for such a time as this.

Perhaps this is the moment for which you have been created.

...for such a time as this.

Perhaps this is the moment for which you have been created.

...for such a time as this.

Perhaps this is the moment for which you have been created.

...for such a time as this.

Perhaps this is the moment for which you have been created.

...for such a time as this.

Perhaps this is the moment for which you have been created.

...for such a time as this.

Perhaps this is the moment for which you have been created.

...for such a time as this.

Perhaps this is the moment for which you have been created.

...for such a time as this.

Perhaps this is the moment for which you have been created.

...for such a time as this.

Perhaps this is the moment for which you have been created.

...for such a time as this.

Perhaps this is the moment for which you have been created.

...for such a time as this.

Perhaps this is the moment for which you have been created.

...for such a time as this.

Perhaps this is the moment for which you have been created.

...for such a time as this.

Perhaps this is the moment for which you have been created.

...for such a time as this.

Perhaps this is the moment for which you have been created.

...for such a time as this.

Perhaps this is the moment for which you have been created.

...for such a time as this.

Perhaps this is the moment for which you have been created.

...for such a time as this.

Perhaps this is the moment for which you have been created.

...for such a time as this.

Perhaps this is the moment for which you have been created.

...for such a time as this.

Perhaps this is the moment for which you have been created.

...for such a time as this.

Perhaps this is the moment for which you have been created.

...for such a time as this.

Perhaps this is the moment for which you have been created.

...for such a time as this.

Perhaps this is the moment for which you have been created.

...for such a time as this.

Perhaps this is the moment for which you have been created.

...for such a time as this.

Perhaps this is the moment for which you have been created.

...for such a time as this.

Perhaps this is the moment for which you have been created.

...for such a time as this.

Perhaps this is the moment for which you have been created.

...for such a time as this.

Perhaps this is the moment for which you have been created.

...for such a time as this.

Perhaps this is the moment for which you have been created.

...for such a time as this.

SEE OUR LARGE SELECTION OF JOURNALS ON AMAZON.
WWW.AMAZON.COM/AUTHOR/ROGENAMITCHELLJONES

Rogena Mitchell-Jones
rmj JOURNALS
www.rogenamitchell.com

FOR BULK ORDERS, CONTACT THE AUTHOR AT
ROGENA@ROGENAMITCHELL.COM

RMJ JOURNALS IS AN IMPRINT OF
RMJ MANUSCRIPT SERVICE LLC
ROGENA MITCHELL-JONES, LITERARY EDITOR
WWW.ROGENAMITCHELL.COM

FOCUSING ON THE ART OF EDITING
rmj manuscript service
Rogena Mitchell-Jones

A Professional Editing Service | Freelance Editing with Affordable Rates
Striving for Excellence for You, the Author, Providing Concise Literary & Technical Editing.

...for such a time as this.

"Having worked as a screenwriter for 31 years, I was worn out by countless battles with clueless development execs who wanted to weigh in on how to 'fix' my screenplays, so I was nervous about hiring an 'editor' to help me refine my first novel. It was my experience that those who could actually write, wrote; those who couldn't write, edited. Rogena changed all that. Frankly, I wouldn't publish a thing without her.

"She was forceful with her criticisms without being intractable. She was collaborative without being pedantic, and most importantly, she took the time to analyze, understand and respect my unique style without trying to impose her own. She's an ace with punctuation, something we ignore in screenwriting, and she's a wiz at formatting, making the "e" in e-book stand for 'easy.'

"I am deeply indebted to her and remain one of her biggest fans. Honestly, if there's anything in my book you don't like, I'd bet real money that it's an instance where I ignored Rogena's advice. That's how good she is."

Kevin Alyn Elders is an Author, Screenwriter, Producer, and Director. From his early works, including the Iron Eagle action adventure series, through his later works, including Echelon Conspiracy, he has sold 23 out of 26 original screenplays and has written in many genres for notable directors, actors and producers such as Oliver Stone, Sean Connery, Sylvester Stallone, Arnold Schwarzenegger, Joel Silver, Albert S. Ruddy, and Louis Gossett Jr. His taut, compelling, suspense-filled narratives have found their latest incarnation in his upcoming Screen Novel Series of Paperbacks, EBooks, and Audiobooks. www.kevinalynelders.com.

* * * * *

"On the shore, there was a voice of reason. It was a voice who spoke of telling a story, not about gerunds and gerundives. It spoke of the power of words strung together, not only to convey a concept, but also to tell a story, to draw forth from the reader their untold, unrealized story. And the voice was Rogena Mitchell-Jones."

BAER CHARLTON, AUTHOR OF THE PULITZER PRIZE NOMINATED BOOK, STONEHEART: A PATH OF IDENTITY AND REDEMPTION

RMJ MANUSCRIPT SERVICE

A PROFESSIONAL EDITING SERVICE | FREELANCE EDITING WITH AFFORDABLE RATES

STRIVING FOR EXCELLENCE FOR YOU, THE AUTHOR, PROVIDING CONCISE LITERARY & TECHNICAL EDITING.

"MY NAME IS ROGENA, AND I AM A BOOKAHOLIC."

THE FIRST STEP IS ADMISSION, RIGHT? OK, SERIOUSLY.

Currently, Rogena Mitchell-Jones lives in South Jersey with her wife, Karen, and their extremely pampered cats. If she isn't at home editing or reading, you might find her on the beach—book in hand.

Her background consists of over 25 years in journalism and now editing full time for independent authors internationally since 2013. Her clientele base includes a vast array of Amazon, USA Today, and NY Times Best Selling Authors.

The end of 2014, Rogena was nominated as best editor in an awards event sponsored by The Kindle Hub—TKH Book Awards 2014. With nearly sixty editors competing, she advanced to the finals and came in second in the final competition. With the title of BEST EDITOR 2014 Finalist, it shows hard work does pay off.

She isn't a writer. She's an editor. She is here because she wants to assist you, the author, in creating a manuscript free of typographical errors, including misspelled words, grammatical errors, and inconsistencies in plot and characters.

She gives attention to detail. With this attention to detail, she is able to polish your future best seller, like polishing fine silver that once belonged to your grandmother. Let's make your manuscript the masterpiece you have dreamed of publishing.

She is an editor, not an author. She is a reader, not a writer. She is a Copy Editor. She wants to live in your story while reading your manuscript.

She is here to assist you so you will have a result allowing your future readers to enjoy your published work.

Contact her on Facebook or via email at rogena@rogenamitchell.com.

ROGENA MITCHELL-JONES MANUSCRIPT SERVICE
WWW.ROGENAMITCHELL.COM

Made in the USA
Coppell, TX
31 July 2021